KICK-ASS 2 PRELUDE:
HIT-GIRL

KICK-ASS 2 PRELUDE: HIT-GIRL. MOVIE COVER ISBN: 9781783290109. DIRECT MARKET ISBN: 9781783290116. Contains material originally published in magazine form as HIT-GIRL #1-5. Published by Titan Books, a division of Titan Publishing Group Ltd., 144 Southwark St., London, SE1 0UP. Copyright © 2010-2013 Millarworld Limited and John S. Romita. All Rights Reserved. "Kick-Ass", "Kick-Ass 2", "Hit-Girl", the Kick-Ass, Hit-Girl, and Kick-Ass 2 logos, and all prominent characters and their likenesses featured herein are trademarks of Millarworld Limited & John S. Romita. "Millarworld" and the Millarworld logo are trademarks of Millarworld Limited. No part of this publication may be reproduced, stored in a retrieval system, or transmitted, in any form or by any means, without the prior written permission of Millarworld Limited, John S. Romita, or the publisher. Names, characters, places, and incidents featured in this publication are either the product of the author's imagination or used fictitiously. Any resemblance to actual persons, living or dead (except for satirical purposes), is entirely coincidental. Visit www.millarworld.tv.

A CIP catalogue record for this title is available from the British Library.

First edition: August 2013

1 3 5 7 9 10 8 6 4 2

Printed in Spain

KICK-ASS 2 PRELUDE:

HIT-GIRL

Writer & Co-Creator
MARK MILLAR

Breakdowns & Co-Creator
JOHN ROMITA JR.

Finishes & Ink Washes
TOM PALMER

Colourist
DEAN WHITE
with MICHAEL KELLEHER

Letterer
CHRIS ELIOPOULOS

Editor
JENNIFER LEE

Collection Editor: **JENNIFER LEE**

Book Designer: **SPRING HOTELING**

SVP of Print & Digital Publishing Sales: **DAVID GABRIEL**

SVP of Operations & Procurement, Publishing: **DAVID BOGART**

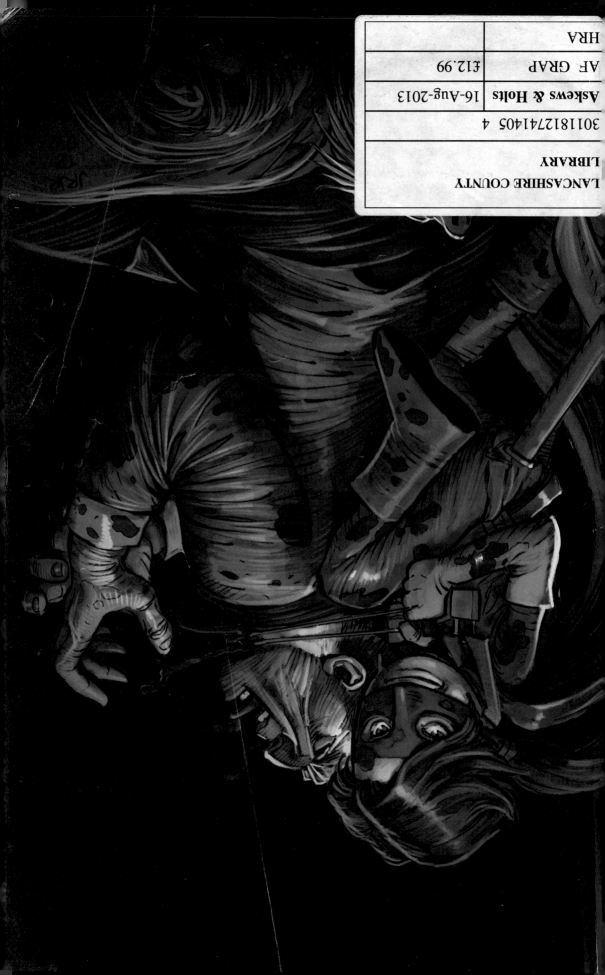

I am writing this to you from Mark Millar's dank, Scottish cellar. He says if I don't keep typing, he's going to turn on those jumper cables he's got hooked up to my balls! He went for a pint though, so please, I have seconds, seconds only! Someone send help! Please, I hear him coming bac—

ZZZttt!!!

Aagh!!

So, maybe that's not exactly true. Maybe I'm actually writing this from the comfort of my desk in Long Island. But you'd believe it, right? It's exactly the sort of thing you expect from a man who's written more gut-wrenching ultraviolence, more earth-shaking action than anyone I know. Hell, it's the kind of thing I expected, too, when I first met him.

Which brings me to London, spring 2012. I was there for my first Kapow!Con, and I had barely dropped off my bags when I got a text from Mark, asking me to come meet him for a drink. We had chatted through emails a bit in the weeks leading up to the convention, but I'd never met the man face-to-face. I was nervous. I half expected to walk up to the convention center and see some douchebag come flying through the glass, Mark stepping out after him, swords strapped on, pint in hand, delivering some awesome quip in a growling brogue before chopping the guy's feet off.

But that's not the man I found sitting there at the café by the convention offices. The man I found, Mark Millar, was cradling and feeding his newborn daughter, sipping at a coffee. As soon as he saw me he smiled and waved me over. "Young man!" he said, offering me a seat.

You can probably guess this initial meeting didn't end with the death of untold hundreds. It was really just a great conversation. I have young children myself, and so we got lost for a while, trading stories about these beautiful kids who keep us up all night like fucking maniacs, but whom we love more than the world. Honestly, it surprised me a little, how open and down-to-earth Mark was from go, and above all, how heartfelt his conversation was. Thinking back now, though, I know it shouldn't have surprised me. Because the ugly truth is that at its core, for me, Mark's work has always been about heart.

Now I can hear you out there: "Heart? Fuck off Snyder!" But hear me out...

Because for me, what makes Mark's work beloved by fans around the world isn't really the ball-zapping thrills or the incredible action. It's his love for his characters. It's the way he makes you relate to and care deeply about each of his creations from the first turn of the page. The craftsmanship in each voice, the quirks in each character's thinking—Mark makes his characters' hearts beat for you, makes them live for you in the most immediate, gripping ways. Better than just about anyone. So at the risk of offending you guys (and maybe even you, Mark), I'd say that at the very heart of Mark's work is, well... heart. Yes, this book has the hyper-violent awesomeness you want and expect from Mark (wait 'til you get to the teddy-bear execution!)… but the magic of the book is how Mark brings to life Mindy's everyday problems side-by-side with the badassery. Here, in HIT-GIRL, we see her vulnerable for the first time, really vulnerable. Don't get me wrong, this is the Mindy you know and love—the vigilante, raised to be the toughest, deadliest hero in the world. But it's also Mindy the kid, trying to figure out how to be child, a daughter, a friend… a Mindy I'm sure you'll come to know and love even more.

Now if Mark's writing is the heart of this book, then John Romita Jr.'s storytelling is its soul. After all, what awesome thing is there to say about his work that hasn't been said before? His signature style is here in all its glory, so expressive and dynamic. His storytelling has never been better than it is in HIT-GIRL. And of course, here there's an extra thrill of getting to see him cut loose, shake off the restraints of all things kid-friendly, and get totally down and dirty. You can just tell from the art how much fun he's having, and it makes for an incredible read. And there's no overestimating the contribution of the crew John has with him here. Between Tom Palmer's rich line-work and finishes, Dean White's evocative colors and Chris Eliopoulos' artful lettering, you've got one of the best teams in visual storytelling.

So friends, to finish up, what follows here is a great book, by a great team, featuring the most bad-ass character currently in comics… There's no way you can read this book and not get swept away by the characters, the mindblowing action, and the adoration of comics inherent on every page. Because, like all the KICK-ASS books, this one is also about the transformative power of comics, about their ability to inspire wonder and desires—good and bad. Like I said, it's a book made with much love, and I couldn't be more honored that Mark decided to reach out to me to write this. Savor this book; it's a wonder.

Still, the next time Mark invites me for a drink, he better bring his fucking swords. Swords, Mark!

Scott Snyder is a novelist and the award-winning writer for BATMAN, SWAMP THING, SEVERED, and AMERICAN VAMPIRE.

ONE

Must be *somebody* knows who these two cocksuckers really are.

So what do we do now?

I dunno. Hang around the bad areas and try to catch *another* one, I guess.

Apologies.

What's the matter with you, Michael? You almost ruined *my shoes,* you fucking animal!

FUCK!

TWO

THREE

UNG!

What the hell?

Are you okay?

I-I'm fine. I just...

THAT GUY JUST SHOT OUR DAD!

What?

It's okay! I got him!

Get off me, you idiot!

What the hell? Were you just watching me use the *bathroom,* you lesbian?

"Wake up, bitch.

"C'mon. I didn't haul your ass up here so you could take a *nap.*"

Wh-What?

Wh-Where am I? I...

Mindy's House:

Hey, honey. What's up?

You *lied* to me, Marcus. You said they weren't *leaning* on you, but look what just got delivered. It says *Mommy Bear*, *Daddy Bear* and *Baby Bear* on them...

Oh, Jesus.

The Police Department:

Gigante, I need to *talk* to you.

5TH PRECINCT

An abandoned building with a new ventilation system should be enough to alert the boys in blue that there's something GOING ON.

But the cops don't want to know. Not as long as they're getting their kickback from UNCLE GODDAMN RALPHIE.

I planned to tie the exits shut and torch the entire building, but I didn't count on so many GIRLS working here.

Some of them don't look much older than ME.

Hey, Rudy. Go get us another *bottle*.

Whatever you say, Spoons.

Eight different HEAVIES in his inner circle. All well-built and armed to the teeth.

Why the hell did you have to stand me up TONIGHT, Kick-Ass?

Guess I should be *sensible* and head outside.

Wait for them across the street and pick them off with my *sniper rifle* before anyone even...

Yes, of *course* I know about the blaze on TV now and working out how much goddamn *money* this is costing me.

Believe me, boss. We're trying our best to get to the bottom of it, but nobody knows a *thing* about this kid.

We snatched another *super* off the street, but it's just like those *other* clowns. He's literally *never met* her.

It doesn't matter. This has nothing to do with the superheroes. I don't care *what* the workers think they saw.

Marcus Williams was leading that raid last night and I've started to wonder if he might be behind all our *other* problems lately.

Now, he could be working for a rival gang or he's maybe just a *conscientious cop.* Either way, he ignored our warning and and needs to be made an *example* of.

FIVE

Marcus is the closest thing I have to a *dad* now, shithead. He's so good to Mom I could *cry* sometimes...

...this is for sticking a *gun* in his face.

Nice job, baby-doll. But what do you do *now*?

I'd spent *weeks* coming up with the coolest deaths and funny little quips as I finished them off.

I crossed the city like a fucked-up Santa, sliding down chimneys and dispensing death like candy canes.

I nixed them all in a single night and don't know how I did it, but I hadn't had this much fun since Daddy gave me that *terrorist* to play with on my eighth birthday.

Strangled. Decapitated. Blown to pieces with *grenades* up their asses. It was *awesome.*

But the boss I saved for *last.* The guy who thought he was safe up there in his *big castle.*

Mom and Marcus were still out cold when I got back home, and just like I hoped, Marcus took *the blame* for me.

He told his friends it was self-defense, and all the other cops figured he'd probably get a *medal* for defending his home against four armed intruders.

I just never expected *Mom* to be so freaked out. I never knew how *fragile* she was until I saw her shaking and crying in the middle of the garden.

But Marcus was *amazing*. He'd been helping her through her *anxiety attacks* and knew exactly what to do to get her breathing under *control*.

That's when I realized that Marcus was right and Mom could never know the truth about my Hit-Girl past.

The idea that her *husband* had taken four lives almost pushed her over the edge.

What would she do if she ever found out I had over *a hundred kills* under my utility belt?

Do you understand *why* this has to stop now?

Relax, Marcus. It's over. We're safe now *anyway*.

The local Mafia pulled right back, shell-shocked and disorientated.

Their leaders were gone, their soldiers in retreat and Marcus was no longer in danger now that *Genovese* had been taken down.

I hung up my cape and focused on school-work, but as rumors spread of what happened that night it had never been more *fashionable* to be out there in a pair of pantyhose.

Brand new heroes were appearing every day and the Twitter-sphere was blazing with *team-up* talk and *super-groups* and all these things I so *desperately* wanted.

But it wasn't just the *heroes* who were getting their asses organized.

Red Mist's video had gone seriously viral and every little prick with a history of self-harm suddenly had a *figurehead*.

Kung-Fu School, Asia:

END OF BOOK TWO

MARK MILLAR has written some of Marvel's greatest modern hits including *The Ultimates, Ultimate X-Men, Spider-Man, Wolverine: Old Man Logan,* and *Civil War,* the industry's biggest-selling series of the last decade. His Millarworld line boasts a roster of creator-owned smashes such as *Wanted,* turned into a blockbuster movie starring Angelina Jolie; *Kick-Ass,* which starred Nicolas Cage; and *Kick-Ass 2,* starring Jim Carrey. Millar is currently working on *Kick-Ass 3, Jupiter's Legacy,* and *Nemesis Returns.* In his native UK, he's the editor of *CLiNT* magazine, an advisor on film to the Scottish government, and CEO of film and TV company Millarworld Productions. He also serves as Creative Consultant on Fox's Marvel movies in Los Angeles.

JOHN ROMITA JR is a modern-day comic-art master, following in his legendary father's footsteps. Timeless runs on *Iron Man, Uncanny X-Men, Amazing Spider-Man,* and *Daredevil* helped establish him as his own man artistically, and his work on *Wolverine* and *World War Hulk* is arguably the most explosive comic art of the last decade. In addition to *Eternals* with writer Neil Gaiman, JRJR teamed with Mark Millar on the creator-owned *Kick-Ass,* later developed into a blockbuster feature film starring Nicolas Cage. Avid Spider-Man fans rejoiced at the artist's return to *Amazing Spider-Man* with the Brand New Day storylines "New Ways To Die" and "Character Assassination." He later joined writer Brian Michael Bendis on the relaunched *Avengers.* Recent titles include the blockbuster crossover *Avengers vs X-Men* and the relaunch of *Captain America.*

TOM PALMER has worked as an illustrator in the advertising and editorial fields, but has spent the majority of his career in comic books. His first assignment, fresh out of art school, was on *Doctor Strange.* He has since gone on to lend his inking talents to many of Marvel's top titles, including *X-Men, The Avengers, Tomb of Dracula,* and more recently *Punisher, Hulk,* and *Ghost Rider.* He lives and works in New Jersey.

DEAN WHITE is one of the comic industry's best and most sought-after color artists. Well-known for his work on titles such as *The Amazing Spider-Man*, *Punisher*, *Dark Avengers*, *Captain America*, *Black Panther*, *Wolverine*, and countless more, Dean's envelope-pushing rendering and color palette bring a sense of urgency and power to every page he touches.

CHRIS ELIOPOULOS is a multiple award-winner for his lettering, having worked on dozens of books during the twenty years he's been in the industry — including Erik Larsen's *Savage Dragon*, for which he hand-lettered the first 100 issues. Adding to his success as a letterer, he also publishes his own strip *Misery Loves Sherman*, wrote and illustrated the popular *Franklin Richards: Son of a Genius* one-shots, and wrote Marvel's *Lockjaw and the Pet Avengers* series.

JENNIFER LEE is a story editor and producer working across film, comics, and prose. She's edited for both Marvel and DC Comics, and her books include *Daredevil, Black Widow, 100 Bullets, Transmetropolitan*, and the award-winning illustrated prose novel *The Sandman: The Dream Hunters*. *Hit-Girl* marks Jenny's reunion with Mark Millar and John Romita Jr, whom she edited during their seminal run on *Wolverine*. Film credits include *True Adolescents* starring Mark Duplass and Melissa Leo; *Small, Beautifully Moving Parts*; *Union Square* starring Mira Sorvino and Tammy Blanchard; *Arcadia* starring John Hawkes; and *The Skeleton Twins* starring Kristen Wiig and Bill Hader. She lives in New York with her husband, comics illustrator Cliff Chiang.

VARIANT COVERS

FOUR

FOUR

(VARIANT BY GEOF DARROW & PETER DOHERTY)

WORLD™
COLLECTION

MILLAR & McNIVEN'S
NEMESIS

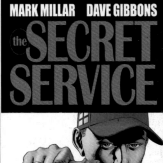

MARK MILLAR   DAVE GIBBONS
the SECRET SERVICE

$2.99

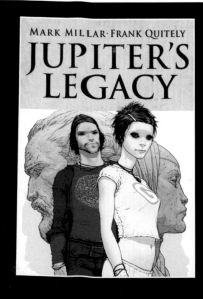

MARK MILLAR · FRANK QUITELY
JUPITER'S LEGACY

AMERICAN JESUS

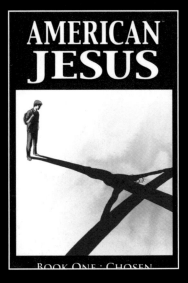

BOOK ONE · CHOSEN

MARK MILLAR   LEINIL YU
SUPER CROOKS

THE HEIST

KICK-ASS
READING ORDER

PART ONE

KICK-ASS

NOW A MAJOR MOTION PICTURE!

MARK MILLAR
JOHN ROMITA JR.

PART TWO

KICK-ASS 2 PRELUDE

HIT-GIRL

MARK MILLAR
JOHN ROMITA JR.
TOM PALMER and DEAN WHITE

PART THREE

KICK-ASS 2

MARK MILLAR
JOHN ROMITA JR.

PART FOUR

KICK-ASS 3

**THE GRAND
FINALE**

MAY 2013